Bottles & cans

using them again

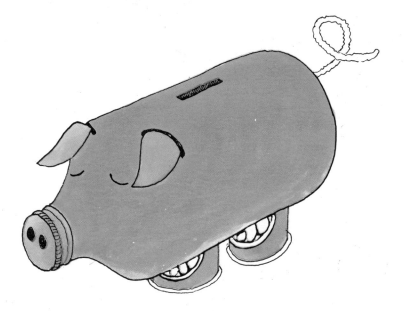

A Puffin Book
Written and produced by McPhee Gribble Publishers
Illustrated by David Lancashire

About bottles and cans

No one can avoid bottles and cans. They line the shelves of supermarkets and most other kinds of shops. They lie by our roadsides and on river beds and on the sea floor.

Almost everything we eat, drink, or put on ourselves is packed in plastic or glass or cans made of aluminum or steel.

Once people went to a grocer's shop and watched the grocer weigh out their sugar, flour, raisins and salt, then wrap them in strong paper bags. Sometimes they took along their own containers and filled them up with nails or honey or oil.

A lot of things were made at home – like candles, cheese, soap and crackers. Fruit was stored for the winter and meat was pickled to last.

The way we live now doesn't leave much time for growing and storing food for each family. Many people don't know how or haven't the space, so we buy things that have been made in factories and packed in containers.

NEW

FRUTO

FARM FRESH FRUIT DRINK

ARTIFICIALLY FLAVORED AND COLORED

bottles and cans are made to look good so we will buy more

Every year people use billions of cans and billions of glass bottles and plastic containers that nobody wants again. Most of them end up in city rubbish dumps or are left lying around.

Bottles and aluminum cans don't rot so they are there forever. This is a huge problem that worries a lot of people.

The makers of throw-away containers are beginning to understand the trouble they cause.

It is a nuisance collecting bottles, washing them and refilling them, relabeling them and selling them again. Some makers do this–but most don't want to.

Others are trying ways to use the metal from old cans to make new ones. This is called recycling. But most people don't care and just dump bottles and cans anyway.

There are dozens of ways that packaging can be used again. Some people are even working on low cost housing made out of things that are usually dumped.

There are many things you can do. Best of all, try not to buy things packed in containers that can't be returned and reused. Or you could take all your plastic bottles and cans and glass bottles back to the makers or to the shops – but they are usually just dumped in the end.

You can reuse a lot of packaging too. Collect bottles and cans that are lying around and make things out of them. This is what this book is all about.

Warnings

Make sure that all containers you want to use are safe. Read the labels before you start. Many things are poisonous.

Containers that have had medicines or garden mixtures or heating fuel in them should not be used again.

Old bottles or cans that have had strange things in them should never be used either. Odd smells or stains are danger signs.

Wash cans and bottles that have held food or drink in hot soapy water. Rinse them well. If you are going to use them for food or drink get advice before you start.

Only make things from cans that are already open. Closed cans with spray tops must never be used. They can explode.

spray cans are packed with gas – never use them again

Cutting and decorating

Some cans are made of steel and some are made of aluminum. Some have tops that take off with a can opener. Most drink cans have tops you pull out or punch in.

Cans can be cut with tin snips and wire cutters – but this is difficult. You also end up with an edge sharp enough to slice you. So don't bother with cutting cans unless you want one for a special job – and then get someone to help you.

Cans can be painted with house paint. You can glue paper or felt on them to decorate them.

There are many different kinds of plastic too. Some can be cut with scissors – the thin plastic you can bend easily. Others need a sharp knife with a point to make the first hole. A bread knife makes a good saw if you don't need a neat edge. Draw a pencil line to help you cut straight.

Plastic bottles can be painted or drawn on with felt pens if they are not very shiny. You can glue paper shapes on them too.

Some people cut glass bottles by tying a hot wire tightly where the break is wanted. The bottle is dipped quickly into cold water to crack at the heated line.

Even experts have trouble making this work. So don't try it – use glass bottles whole.

Most paper labels will peel off bottles and cans if you soak them in warm water. Hard scrubbing with a pot scourer gets rid of most glue marks. A little alcohol on a rag can help.

Pet water supply

You need a can, a saucer, a hammer and a fat nail to make holes in the can.

Stand the open end of the can in the saucer and mark where the water will come up to when the saucer is full.

Now punch one hole in each side of the can just below the water line you have marked.

Fill the can with water, put the saucer over the top and turn the whole thing carefully upside down.

nail hole

water trickles into the saucer each time the pet drinks

Stilts

These are good for seeing over crowds.

Make 2 holes in 2 large cans at the sides near the closed ends. Thread long strong pieces of string through them. The string should be about as tall as you.

pull the strings tight as you walk

Candle molds

Make fat lacy candles in 2 small cans.
You will need some ice cubes, 2 thin
candles for wicks, a pound of wax and
a large wax crayon for color.

Melt the crayon and the wax together.

① oil inside the cans then pack ice cubes around the candles

② fill the cans with melted wax

③ open the bottoms of the cans when the wax is hard

④ push the lacy candles out

Can telephone

Sound travels much better along a tight
string than it does through the air.

Find 2 cans open at one end, and a long
piece of strong string about 10 yards long.

make a nail hole in each can

nail hole

thread the string through the nail holes and knot the ends

get a friend to talk into one can — you listen at the other end

the string must be tight and not touching anything

Candle holder

A bottle with a wide neck makes a windproof candle holder.

Tie a piece of string around the neck to make a carrying handle. Stand the candle in a lump of plasticine – or drip some melted wax into the bottom of the bottle to hold the candle in place.

Plant water bottle

Plants need a lot of water if the summers are long and hot where you live. You might not be able to hose them each night – if you are away from home or if your water supply is running low.

This water bottle keeps roots of plants damp for several days. Fill the bottle and push it deep into the soil next to the plant. The water seeps out slowly.

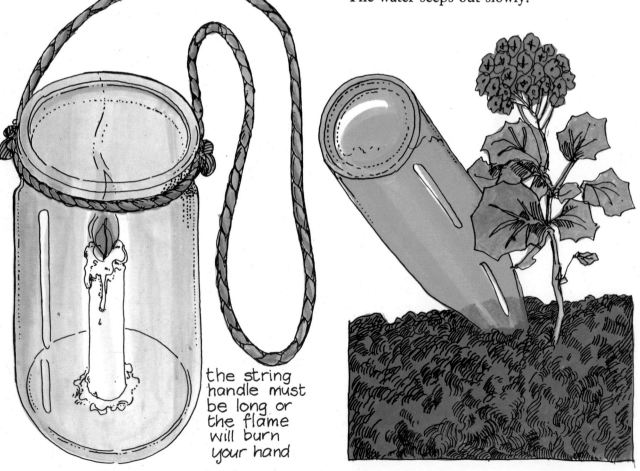

the string handle must be long or the flame will burn your hand

Fishing float

Tie a plastic bottle to your fishing line.
Make sure the lid is on tight. Leave enough
line to dangle a short way above where you
guess is the bottom of the river or pond.

The bottle floats because it is full of air.
A hooked fish won't be able to pull it
under water. You can go off and do other
things.

Pet hot water bottle

Pets get cold on winter nights – especially if
they are new-born or sick.

Fill a bottle with hot water. Screw the top
on tightly and wrap it in something furry.
People like hot water bottles too.

Plastic bottle shapes

Scoops of different sizes can be cut from plastic bottles. Make them for the kitchen or for shoveling sand or earth in a garden.

Mark the shape you need with a pencil line. Saw along the line with a bread knife.

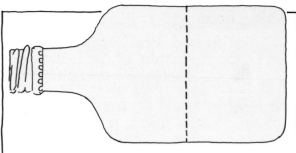

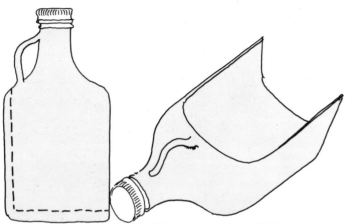

Funnels are for pouring things into jars or bottles with narrow necks. Make a cut through the middle of a plastic bottle. This gives you a funnel that won't easily overflow.

All boats should have a baler tied on firmly for scooping water out fast. Use a plastic bottle with a handle for the rope – and leave the top on.

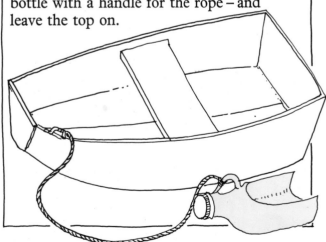

make a collection
of funnels from
big to very small
to give away

Make an automatic pet feeder for animals or birds that eat seed. Find 2 large plastic bottles. Cut the bottom off one to make a bowl. Cut the other almost through like this to make a lid on the feeder.

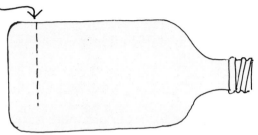

Join the feeder to the side of a cage or fence with 2 loops of wire. The bottle neck should be just a little above the bottom of the bowl – so the seed won't all run out at once.

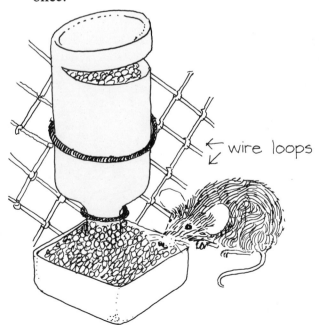

← wire loops

With a collection of large plastic bottles make a row of planters. The tops can make hanging gardens.

Hammer a few nail holes in the bottoms of the bottles to let out drips. The hanging gardens can be nailed to a fence or wall.

Put some pebbles in the bottom of the containers. Then fill them up with potting compost from a garden shop.

put large pebbles in the bottle neck to stop the compost falling out

Puppets

Small plastic juice or cream bottles can make puppet heads.

A handkerchief or a small scarf lets you use fingers for arms. Have 2 rubber bands to put round your thumb and 2 fingers to make arms for the puppet.

Paint the face or draw it on with felt pens. Glue on something for hair too if you like.

Use a small bottle as a base if you want to make a face with a pointy nose.

Get some paste and tear up lots of pieces of paper. Newspaper will do.

Cover the bottle in paste and stick a layer of paper pieces all over it. Then several more layers of paper and paste to get the shape you want. You can start building up the pointed nose now.

Paint the head with water paints when it is quite dry.

Choose a voice for a puppet quite different from your own. That way people won't notice it is you speaking.

hair can be wool or rags or strips of paper

2 fingers in here

thumb in here

GLUE

don't paint the head until it is dry

Piggy bank

A fat plastic bottle and 2 small cans make a large piggy bank. The bottle should have a lid to stop the money falling out.

With a pencil trace around the tops of the cans on to the side of the bottle. Cut around the marks carefully with a sharp knife.

Cut a slit in the other side wide enough to take the biggest coin you have where you live.

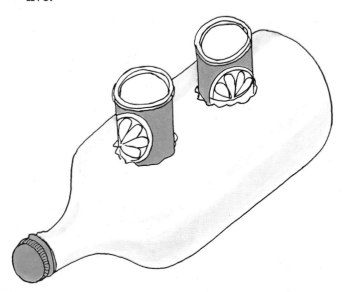

Push the 2 cans into their holes. They should be a tight fit. Push them in straight so that the pig will stand up without wobbling.

Draw on eyes and holes for the nose on the lid. You can cut slits for a tail and ears made of paper if you like. The pig can be painted too.

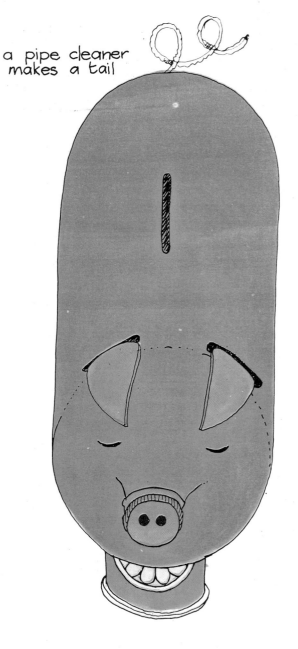

a pipe cleaner makes a tail

When you want to get some money out just pull off one of the legs.

Can cooking

Ever since cans were first invented people have cooked in them. They make good camping gear.

Cans with tight fitting lids keep food dry and fresh. Make sure the cans you use are clean and not rusty.

A billy can is used for making drinks and stews and for boiling water. No good camp should be without one.

Make a billy from a large steel can. Hammer holes for a handle made of bent wire. The holes should be close to the open end. Bend the ends over so the handle is firmly on.

Stir any thick mixtures you cook in a billy – cans are not as heavy as saucepans and mixtures burn easily.

A shallow frying pan can be made from a flat tin. Bend a long thick piece of wire around to make a handle. Wrap some string around the handle – it gets very hot.

You can warm food over a candle standing in a can.

make rough cuts around the top with a can opener

make air holes near the bottom with a nail

If you have a large enough steel can you could make you own outdoor cooker. This gives you an almost instant burner for a hot snack.

A 16oz. fruit can open at one end will do.

Get someone to make 2 holes in it with tin snips. One makes the smoke hole and the other lets you light a tiny fire inside the can.

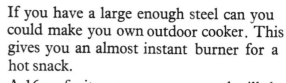

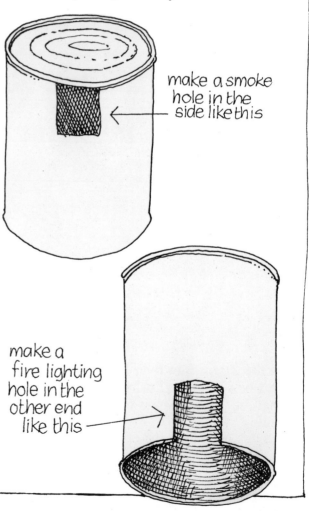

make a smoke hole in the side like this

make a fire lighting hole in the other end like this

a plastic bottle makes a water carrier

a billy can is easily made

make sure everything you use is clean

keep adding small sticks to the fire in the can cooker

wrap string around the wire handle

Music making

Bottles and cans can make music because they are hollow. You can put things like small pebbles or water in them to make different noises.

You can make a banjo with a large plastic bottle and strings of nylon fishing line. Cut a tight hole in the bottle to push a wooden arm through. You'll need screw eyes at each end for the strings. Put a matchbox between the strings and the bottle to tighten them.

a large can or plastic bottle makes a drum

shake pebbles or beans inside plastic bottles for rhythm

nail bottle tops loosely in heaps to a broom handle for a tambourine stick

a piece of tube can go over the neck of half a plastic bottle for trumpet noises

play on glass bottles filled with water of different heights for different sounds

an old fork would do

cut the bottom out of a plastic bottle and sing through it

Gardens in bottles and cans

Grow plants indoors in a large clear plastic or glass bottle. The plants keep themselves moist and don't take much looking after.

Choose a fat bottle with quite a narrow neck. Wash it well before you start.

Make a bottle gardening tool from a small spoon tied to the end of a long stick.

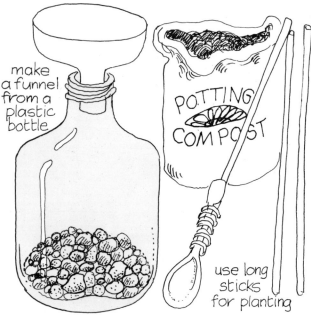

make a funnel from a plastic bottle

POTTING COMPOST

use long sticks for planting

You will need potting compost from a garden shop to grow the plants in. Ordinary garden soil won't do. Plants need lots of rich food to grow well in a small space.

Put a layer of clean pebbles in the bottom of the bottle. Then pour in a layer of potting mix about 1½ inches deep. Sprinkle in a little charcoal if you can find some. This keeps the soil sweet.

All kinds of small plants will grow in a bottle garden. Collect them and have them ready to plant at the same time.

Try to find some moss growing in your neighborhood. Peel up a small piece and press it firmly on to the compost.

Ferns and small flowering plants such as African violets make good bottle garden plants. Small leafed ivy grows well in a bottle too. Pinch off a healthy shoot. The stem will quickly grow roots when it is stuck in the compost.

take off the bottom leaves and push the ivy stem well down into the compost

Use 2 long sticks to put the plants in their places. Make a hole for plants with roots then ease them gently into it. Cover the roots firmly with compost – use the spoon tool.

After planting is finished sprinkle in some water to dampen the soil. A bottle garden won't need much water after this. Extra water can't escape and will just lie around and become stale.

Keep the bottle in a light room – but not in direct sunshine. A bottle gets hot very quickly and the plants will die.

You can make a whole garden in a collection of cans. Plants in small spaces quickly use up the goodness in garden soil – so buy a bag of potting compost.

Make drainage holes in the bottoms and stand the cans in saucers to catch drips.

Put in a layer of pebbles and then almost fill the cans with potting compost.

Geraniums or bulbs are good for large cans. A flower seedling like a primrose or a pansy grows well in a small can.

keep the cans on a light window sill and water them often

Things in bottles

Clear glass or plastic bottles can be filled with things and decorated.

People long ago worked out ways of painting pictures on the inside of bottles with long brushes. Sailors sometimes built very real-looking sailing ships inside bottles with narrow necks. Some ships took years to build.

Cut shapes like stars and moons out of silver foil and stick them on to the outside of a wide-necked bottle.

Find some shiny balls to hang from the lid inside. Christmas decorations or balls of crumpled foil work well. Put them at different heights so they swing and sparkle.

hang things from string taped to the lid

You can make a world inside a bottle. You will need some plasticine or modeling clay for the ground and some long tools to push things into place. Tweezers, kitchen skewers or long thin sticks will do.

Lie the bottle on its side. Push in some sausage shapes of plasticine or clay.

flatten the ground against the side of the bottle

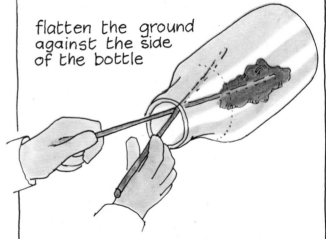

All kinds of things can stand up in the bottle. Slide them in and push them upright with your tools.

Leafy twigs and plastic figures can be pressed into the ground.

Make your own cardboard cutouts too. Stand them on a small lump of plasticine before you slide them into the bottle.

A fleet of little ships can sail in a bottle on a plasticine or paper sea.

Walnut shells or painted bits of egg cartons are good hulls. Put a dob of plasticine inside the hull to hold up the mast. This can be a toothpick with a paper sail.

The mast leans over when it is being slipped into place. Then you push it upright with your long stick.

You can make a snowstorm in a clear bottle with flat sides. Small food flavoring bottles work well.

You will need a packet of silver glitter and some glycerine. Glycerine is thick and clear so the snowflakes drift down.

Draw or find a wintery picture to fit one side of the bottle.

Put about a teaspoonful of glitter into the bottle – enough to cover the bottom with a thin layer.

Add the glycerine carefully until the bottle is three-quarters full. Then fill up the rest of the space with water and screw the lid on tightly.

druggists sell glycerine

Tape the picture to the bottle so it faces in. You look at it through the other side.

Give the bottle a hard shake then hold it still. You will see the picture through a whirling snowstorm.

Games

Bottles and cans can be used for lots of games. You can invent them or copy them from games in shops. Your games can be more interesting than things that cost a lot of money.

A large plastic bottle and a small can make a catching game. Find a bottle with a handle and cut it in half.

Make a nail hole in the can. Join it to the bottle handle with a long piece of string. The longer the string the harder the game.

The game is to hold the neck of the bottle and jerk the can into the air. You try to catch the can in the scoop as many times in a row as possible.

A collection of tall plastic bottles makes bowling pins. Fill them with water or sand so they won't fall over easily. A heavy ball you can bowl slowly works best – a baseball or a hard orange.

line the bottles up and see how many can be knocked over at once

A pyramid of cans can make another kind of game. Paint the cans different colors if you like and fill them with sand so they don't blow away. Each player has 3 throws to knock them down. Stand a good way back to make it harder.

Cans make giant pieces for games like checkers or chess.

you could paint a huge games board on a patch of concrete or on cardboard

small round cans painted black and white make checkers

paint 16 cans black and 16 cans white for a chess set

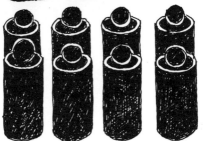

make a big label for each piece — or glue on paper tops and ping pong balls

Jointed things

Drink cans with ring pulls or pop tops
can be joined together with long strings.

You can join them up by making a nail hole
in the bottom of each can. Use a fat nail.
Thread string through the hole and out
through the opening on the top.

You could make a huge jointed giant or a
snake. Or invent your own jointed creature.
Large plastic bottles make bodies and heads.

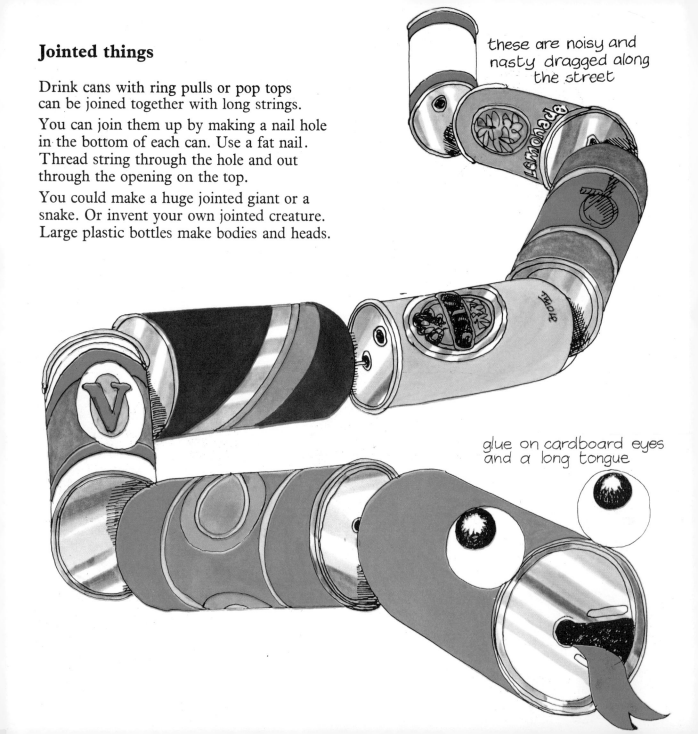

these are noisy and
nasty dragged along
the street

glue on cardboard eyes
and a long tongue

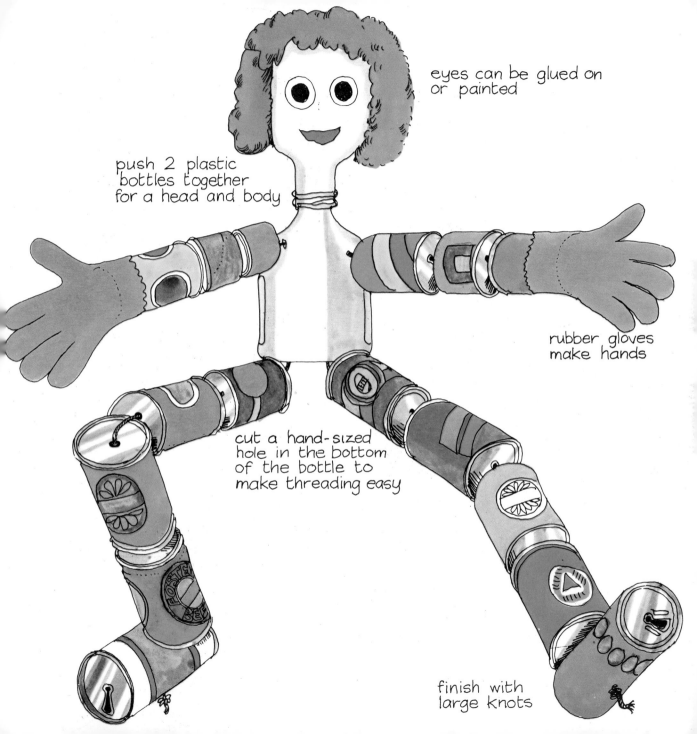

eyes can be glued on or painted

push 2 plastic bottles together for a head and body

rubber gloves make hands

cut a hand-sized hole in the bottom of the bottle to make threading easy

finish with large knots

Home-bottled cordial

Billions of factory-made drinks are swallowed each year. Billions of drink bottles and cans lie around.

Once people made their own drinks with fruit they grew. Cordials were stored in cool stone jars with cork stoppers.

You can make a cordial which will last for a long time. Store it in a large soft-drink bottle with a screw top.

You will need for 1 bottle
1 orange or lemon
2 cups of sugar
3 teaspoons of tartaric acid crystals
2 large cups of boiling water

use a shiny-clean drink bottle

you will need a jug, a bowl and a strainer

Peel the orange or lemon thinly – a potato peeler makes this easy.

The white pith left on the fruit tastes bitter so cut it off. Then slice the bare shiny fruit. Put the slices in a bowl with the peel, sugar and tartaric acid.

tartaric acid is made from green grapes and keeps the cordial fresh

Pour on the boiling water and stir until the grains of sugar dissolve.

Leave the mixture to get cold – overnight if you can.

guess how much for 2 large cups of boiling water

Strain the cold cordial into a jug to take out the peel and fruit. Pour it into a clean bottle and screw the top on firmly.

The cordial is very strong and sweet. Mix it with lots of water and ice.

LEMON CORDIAL

Masks

Large plastic bottles can be used for making masks. They can be cut into odd shapes and have faces painted or glued on them. Hair can be stuck on too.

Make a half mask from half a large bottle. The spout becomes the nose. Cut out eye holes so you can see where you are going. Cut holes in the sides for strings to tie it on.

Masks you hold in one hand are good for quick changes from being one thing to another. You can have several masks working at once.

cut the bottle like this for a spout nose

try different kinds of shapes with other bottles

cut the bottle like this for a mask you hold in your hand

You can use 2 bottles to make a mask.
Cut one longways in half – choose a size
that fits your face.

Cut up the other bottle to make ears. You
cut slits in the sides of the face bottle to
push the ears through.

A large nose can be made by cutting around
the widest part of the neck of the bottle.
Tape it in place or cut slits for it too.

Cut a jagged mouth hole if you want to
speak through it. Don't make the eye holes
too big – just enough to see through. Then
draw large eyes around the holes with felt pens.

Elastic knotted through holes at the sides
keeps the mask in place.

hair can be paper strips taped on

ear

cut a
slit
like this

this bit
holds the
ear on

nose

these tabs
hold the
nose on

cut
4 slits

ears
can be
huge and
painted

Constructions

Bottles and cans can be used for making large constructions. This is not a new idea. People have sometimes built bottle houses or piled up cans joined with cement or mud.

Some planners are working on ideas for re-using bottles and cans for low cost houses for people.

There are many ways bottles and cans could be used for buildings. Steel or aluminium cans have been collected and crushed into sheets of metal. Glass bottles have been broken up and mixed with cement for buildings too.

Cans used whole could make filling for walls and roofs. Hundreds of cans between thin sheets of plastic or board would make very strong constructions.

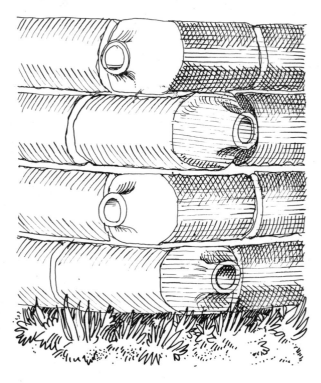

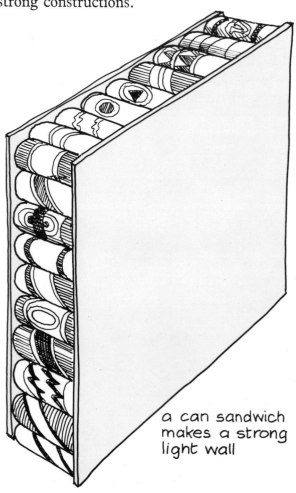

a can sandwich makes a strong light wall

A few years ago a bottle was designed to be re-used as a brick – but we have to get used to ideas like this. Advertising people and makers still think we want throw-away containers.

Building materials cost a lot of money but used cans and bottles are free. Sorting them is the problem. Once they get into rubbish collections they are hard to separate from other things.

It makes sense to build houses out of waste bottles and cans. There are far too many of them lying around the world and not nearly enough houses for people.

You can build large things out of lots of cans. Collect cans the same size and get hold of some very strong glue.

These are some ideas from people who have tried to find new uses for things that nobody wants any more.

Don't leave bottles and cans around

The world is fast running out of wild places where people haven't left their mark. Most places are spoiled by some kind of rubbish.

Glass, plastic, aluminum and steel containers can be found almost everywhere.

They are thrown out of cars or left lying around after picnics. They are dumped in the sea.

These things spoil wild places. They also hurt and kill hundreds of small creatures every year. Animals as well as people can cut themselves. Tiny fish grow too big inside cans to swim out again.

Bottles and cans are often found with small animals dead inside them. They crawled in looking for shelter – but the slippery sides stopped them getting out again. And so they slowly died.